The
Power
of Christ in
Baptism

JOHN KINGSLEY ALLEY

PEACE PUBLISHING

The Grace and Power of Christ in Baptism
Copyright © 2002 by John Kingsley Alley

Published in Australia by:
Peace Publishing
PO Box 10187, Frenchville QLD 4701
Email: mail@peace.org.au
Web: www.peace.org.au

ISBN: 978-1-920780-02-9

Contents

Introduction

Baptism is a wonderful subject for our consideration, and of special importance to *every* Christian . This small book was designed especially to prepare new Christians for baptism by giving them an understanding of what baptism means and of its very great importance for the new Christian.

We have found it effective in our own church to make this message available to every person considering baptism.

The book contains a simple and down to earth statement of those things about baptism that should be known and understood by every Christian believer. The individual pastor, home group leader or discipler, will also be able to take the things laid out in this book and explain them more fully to new believers. This message has been a tremendous aid in preparing new believers for baptism and I felt it was of the mind of Christ to make this material available to others as a resource.

There are two great needs before us; every Christian should see and understand clearly the meaning and power of their own baptism, and every new believer or young Christian should be brought to a joyful, liberating and powerful experience of baptism by better understanding the work and purpose of Christ in baptism. In this matter, churches and gospel workers need to be thoughtful and forthright in their proclamation of the Gospel and what submission to Christ means.

I hope and pray that this booklet will be a genuine blessing to the individual reader and a help in the life of those churches that make use of it.

1
The Origins of Baptism

The origins of Christian Baptism can be traced back to Jewish practices, for they baptised their converts from paganism. Gentile converts to Judaism were not only circumcised (if a male), but also baptised, and there was a particular way in which these baptisms took place. They were to stand in a large pool of water up to their neck and listen to a reading from the law - the great commands of the law. Then at the appropriate moment, this gentile proselyte would plunge himself beneath the water.

For the Jews, this represented a <u>cleansing</u> or a <u>washing</u>. They had been in the practice of doing this whenever someone came from the Godless or unbelieving nations and wanted to be incorporated into the privileges and rites of Judaism as the worship of the true God.

John the Baptist

When John the Baptist came on the scene he shocked his fellow Jews by declaring to them, "You need to be baptised also". Of course the Pharisees, the Sadducees, and others made the complaint "but we're sons of Abraham". John replied, "You're not sons of Abraham. God can raise children out of these stones if Abraham needs more children, but until you produce the fruit of repentance, you're not children of Abraham". The Jewish leaders were offended by him, but John the Baptist was using baptism in a new way, and insisting that the Jews themselves submit to it. His baptism was a baptism of <u>repentance</u>, with his message aimed at people who were already Jews and knew the word of God. This was in fact a preparation for the coming of Jesus. By submitting to baptism they signified they were turning away from their sins, to live a new life in accordance with the Law of God. Thus we read below the words of John the Baptist recorded in Matthew's Gospel, where he takes issue with the hypocrisy of the religious leaders of that time.

> *"Confessing their sins, they were baptised by him in the Jordan River. But when he saw many of the Pharisees and Sadducees coming to where he was baptising, he said to them: 'You brood of vipers! Who warned you to flee from the coming wrath? Produce fruit in keeping with repentance. And do not think you can say to yourselves, 'We have Abraham as our father.' I tell you that out of these stones God can raise up children for Abraham. The axe is already at the root of the trees, and every tree that does not produce good fruit will be cut down and thrown into the fire. "*
>
> Matthew 3:6-10

Christ and His Disciples

When Jesus began his ministry with his disciples, they also practiced baptism. At one stage, John the Baptiser and his disciples, and the disciples of Jesus, were each baptising people in the same vicinity. John was baptising people upon their <u>repentance</u>, but nearby, the disciples of Jesus were baptising with a further purpose. Jesus was also preaching repentance, but his disciples were baptising his followers with the added significance that they were <u>surrendering their lives to the Lordship of Christ</u>: they were coming into submission to a particular master, to a particular teacher, the Lord Jesus Christ.

Christian Baptism

Christian baptism includes <u>each</u> of these three things. Let's note them again: The Jews baptised because it was <u>a cleansing and a washing</u>. John the Baptist baptised because it signified <u>repentance</u> in turning away from sin and the old life. The disciples of Jesus baptised because believers were <u>submitting themselves to the Lordship of Christ</u>. They were his followers.

John's baptism of repentance included the symbol of washing, and Jesus' baptism included both washing and repentance, in surrendering to his Lordship.

Christian baptism includes not only all of these ideas, but much more as well. When we look to the Bible, we find many things said concerning the meaning and significance of Christian baptism. In this booklet we shall consider eight important concepts from the New Testament Scriptures concerning baptism into Christ.

2
Fulfilling Righteousness

"Then Jesus came from Galilee to the Jordan to be baptised by John. But John tried to deter him, saying, 'I need to be baptised by you, and do you come to me?' Jesus replied, 'Let it be so now; it is proper for us to do this to fulfil all righteousness. " Then John consented. Matthew 3:13-15

Jesus came to John the Baptist to be baptised by him. It is important to note that Jesus is the Son of God. He did not need baptism to make him a better person because he already was the Son of God. What is more, Jesus was already a holy person. He was without sin, so therefore didn't need to be baptised to take away any sin. He was already righteous, so did not need baptism to make him more righteous. He did not require washing or repentance. Yet when John the Baptist said, "*I need to be baptised by you. Why do you come to me?*", Jesus replied to him, "*It is fitting for us to fulfill all righteousness*". Another way of translating this same sentence (and the way it is translated in some modern English Bibles) is to say "*It is fitting to do all that God wants us to do.*" Now if Jesus had that understanding of baptism, how much more should you and I have that same attitude. If Jesus says that being baptised is part of fulfilling the righteousness that God requires of us, then you and I need to recognise in these words the will of God. We should not need to go any further to see that God the Father asks it of us.

Listening to His Words

Years ago, as I was looking at this matter in the Scriptures, I knew the time had come for me to make a definite decision concerning my own baptism. I had been brought up in a church where it was taught that baptism was unnecessary, and should not be practiced. This produced in me a personal struggle. One day, sitting down with my Bible, I asked the Lord for a final answer to my dilemma. I said, "Lord, show me in the Bible exactly what you want me to do", and the Lord took me through the passages which I'm about to take you to now. He showed me the significance of them, but brought me to **Matthew 3:15** last of all, where I saw the words of Jesus, "*It is fitting for us to fulfill all righteousness*".

Nothing is more important in our lives than to be yielded and submitted to the will of God. We should always be seeking to know the will of God for our lives, and to actively do his will, with the ability he gives to us by his grace.

Obedience Brings Freedom

Often there are difficulties in the way which hinder us from doing what we know to be right and believe to be God's will, and too often we choose to accept the difficulties and hindrances as a valid reason for not changing our lives and not obeying God. But the wonderful truth is that when we take a step of faith to choose God's way, God's power is released, enabling us to do what he tells us. This is grace, given when we believe and in faith choose to obey.

Unbelief keeps us in bondage, but obedience brings us into freedom.

3

Response to the Gospel

"When the people heard this, they were cut to the heart and said to Peter and the other apostles, 'Brothers, what shall we do?' Peter replied, 'Repent and be baptised, every one of you, in the name of Jesus Christ so that your sins may be forgiven. And you will receive the gift of the Holy Spirit'" Acts 2:37-39

I want you to notice in this passage from Acts Chapter 2 that baptism is an important part of both the proclamation of the Gospel, and of our response to the Gospel. It is the way in which we respond to the Lord and become his followers when we are born again by the power of his grace.

In Acts Chapter 2 you will find a description of the day of Pentecost, when the promised Holy Spirit was poured out on the believers. Peter preached a sermon on that occasion in which he declared to all the Jews who had gathered that Jesus was both Lord and Christ, and though they had crucified him, God had raised Jesus from the dead. Here Peter showed them their guilt and sin. Peter preached *". . . and you, with the help of wicked men, put him to death by nailing him to the cross. But God raised him from the dead . . . " "Therefore let all. . . be assured of this: God has made this Jesus, whom you crucified, both Lord and Christ".* Acts 2:23-24,26

The First Believers

In response to this preaching the people *"were cut to the heart and said to Peter and the other apostles, 'Brothers! What shall we do?' "* Acts 2:37. We can amplify their question as, "Brothers, what shall we do <u>to be saved?</u> ". Peter gave the reply recorded in verse 38, telling them to repent and be baptised, and they would receive the gift of the Holy Spirit.

Bear in mind this was the first day of the Christian era - the day of Pentecost. Jesus had ascended to heaven ten days earlier. He had left instructions for his disciples to wait and pray until they received the promised baptism of the Holy Spirit - *'the power from on high'* (See Acts 1:4,5) This was the day the power came!

Immediately in response to this preaching by Peter, there were three thousand new believers. The people then asked *"What have we got to do to be saved?"* In reply Peter said, *"Repent, and be baptised, every one of you, in the name of Jesus Christ for the forgiveness of your sins; and you will receive the gift of the Holy Spirit. The promise is for you and your children and for all who are far off - for all whom the Lord our God will call. "* Acts 2:38 -39.

God's Word Makes a Claim on You

This is the word of God. The word of God lays a claim on every life including yours. If you want to know the proper response to make to the hearing of the Gospel, it is right here in these verses. This is what your response should be when the Spirit of God comes to you, touches your spirit and makes you alive to God, causing you to want to be obedient to the Lord. It is at this moment you experience what is called 'regeneration'. Your spirit was dead to God, dead in sin, but now has been made alive to God, and you now want to know what to do. God has re-created you alive in Christ and put faith in your heart. You know that Jesus is alive and you believe He is your Saviour. What do you do now?

Here is the answer: First of all, repent of your sin. Before God, you give it up. You face a new direction. You turn your back on the old life and you look toward the new life of living for Christ. Then, having put your faith in Christ and having in your heart repentance towards God, you submit to baptism. *"Repent and be baptised"*, Peter said, *"everyone of you, in the name of Jesus Christ for the forgiveness of your sin. . . "*.

Note however, what comes next in this verse ". . . . *and you will receive the gift of the Holy Spirit.* " The Holy Spirit comes too. It's all part of the package.

Public Evangelism

In a Christian 's spiritual growth there has often been a long period of time between salvation and baptism. A common method of evangelism is for people who have expressed faith in God to be led in a 'sinner's prayer'. They pray, *"I believe that Jesus died for me and I ask Jesus to be my Saviour and to forgive my sins"*. But what is mostly neglected is for these new converts to be taught, there and then, about **baptism and the fullness of the Holy Spirit as the immediate experience intended for the new believer.** In fact, these truths should be part of the gospel message as it is preached!

We wonder why our converts are not strong. It is because they have not been taught about baptism from the very beginning. They were meant to learn about it that very first day. It is all part of being converted to Christ. It is all part of a proper response to the Gospel.

When a preacher presents the Gospel message and invites people to come to the Saviour, how does he go about instructing them to respond? This is done in many different ways. A Pastor might say, *"Now while the organ is playing, and while every head is bowed, come and quietly stand here and we'll pray for you and by faith in Jesus you will be saved. "*

Or some might say, "*While every head is bowed, just slip your hand up where you are, and we'll pray for you.* " But if you go to the Bible asking the question "*Lord, what should people do to respond to the Gospel?*", the answer from Scripture is "***repent and be baptised.***"

But that's not all! In the Church we often take *more* months, or *more* years, to teach people about the Baptism in the Holy Spirit when instead we should be specifically instructing them and praying for them regarding the 'gift of the Spirit' when they first come to the Lord. It's all meant to take place on their first day, or first days, as a new Christian .

Personal Witnessing and Sharing Christ

After Christians have witnessed to someone and they want to receive the Lord Jesus as their Saviour, we should not just say, "*Well, repent of your sin and I'll pray , and Jesus will come into your life*". That much is good, but it is incomplete. We should complete the Gospel offer. We should teach them about baptism, and about the promised Holy Spirit by saying, "*If you want to become a follower of the Lord Jesus, then you must be willing to submit to baptism. This is the outward way in which you are showing a complete giving up of your old life, and your desire to live a new life in Christ. As well as that, you need to be filled with the Holy Spirit, because you need his power to live the new life.* "

By giving them the whole instruction from the beginning, you will have done your part in helping the new believer find the true and full experience of the Christian life. You'll have a sound convert. That's the way things were done in the early church as we see from Acts 8:12, Acts 8:35-38, Acts 10:44-48, Acts 16:31-33, as well as from Acts 2:38. .

Although this is not the way we have been operating, this is the way things were done in the early church under the leadership of the Apostles.

A day is coming again, a day of revival and harvest, when we will stand to preach a Gospel message, invite people to come to Jesus through faith and prayer, and invite them to show immediate obedience and submission to his Lordship by being baptised.

The Many Examples in Scripture

There are many examples in "The Acts of the Apostles" which confirm these truths. On the day of their coming to faith in Christ, new believers were instructed that baptism was the specific way in which they submitted their lives to Christ and embraced the gospel faith. In the New Testament, believing the Gospel and choosing to follow Christ was very much tied in with the act of baptism.

Paul and His Ministry

For example, Paul in Acts 9, was struck by the power of Jesus on the road to Damascus. When in Damascus, Ananias was sent by the Lord Jesus to minister the Gospel to him. As Ananias laid hands on him, Paul received his sight, got up immediately, and was baptised. Lydia (Acts 16) and all the people who were living in her house were converted and baptised on the same day. The Philippian jailer and the members of his family were converted one night (Acts 16:33) and as soon as he had washed the wounds of the apostles, he and his family were baptised. Crispus was the ruler of the Synagogue at Corinth. He and the members of his household believed, and many other Corinthians who heard the Gospel through Crispus, *"believed and were baptised"* Acts 18:8. Paul went to Ephesus and found about a dozen disciples there, but when he questioned them about why there was no evidence of the Holy Spirit in their lives, he discovered that they had only heard of John's baptism of repentance. So he baptised them again. They had been baptised into repentance under the message they had understood, but when Paul taught them about Jesus they were baptised into the Lord Jesus Christ that same day. They spoke in tongues and prophesied, and from that small beginning a mighty church was built in Ephesus.

Philip and the Samaritans

Another response to hearing the Gospel is found in Acts 8:4-25 where we read of a marvellous revival which took place in Samaria through the ministry of a young man named Philip. The people believed Philip as he preached Christ and the good news of the Kingdom of God, and were baptised, both men and women. The Scripture says ". . . *when they believed. . . they were baptised. . .* " Acts 8:12

A further example of a proper New Testament application of the Gospel can be seen in Acts 8:34-38. Philip was called to leave Samaria to travel on a desert road where he saw an Ethiopian man travelling in a chariot. Philip, hearing the man reading from the prophet Isaiah, shared Christ with him. Philip began with the very passage of Scripture he was reading (Isaiah 53:7,8) and told him the good news about Jesus. As they travelled along the road they came to some water and the Ethiopian said, *"Look, here is water. Why shouldn't I be baptised?"* Philip baptised him immediately.

Peter and the Gentiles

Now consider the unusual story of Cornelius in Acts Chapter 10. At the instruction of the Lord, Peter had gone to Cornelius' house This was the first time that the Gospel had been proclaimed specifically to the Gentiles. Up until then, the Gospel had been preached to the Jews and the Samaritans. The things we read about in the book of Acts did not all happen in a few weeks, but over many years. By the time of Acts Chapter 10, numerous years had passed since the Pentecost outpouring mentioned in Chapter 2.

Finally however it was the time in the plan and purpose of God to take the Gospel to the Gentiles, and the Holy Spirit used Peter to do this. Peter would never have thought of such a thing himself, and the Lord had to deal with him about it, for Peter, as a Jew, had a religious and cultural rejection of Gentiles. Peter probably never would have concluded his message with an invitation to his hearers to receive Jesus. If it had been left to Peter he would never have appealed to them by saying, *"Now come to Jesus in repentance and we will baptise you and afterwards lay hands on you to be baptised with the Holy Spirit."* He probably would not have done that because of his strong cultural preconceptions about the acceptability of these people. Instead God interrupted the message: *"While Peter was still speaking these words, the Holy Spirit came on all who heard the message. The circumcised believers who had come with Peter were astonished that the gift of the Holy Spirit had been poured out even on the Gentiles. For they heard them speaking in tongues and praising God."* Acts 10:44-46.

"Then Peter said, 'Can anyone keep these people from being baptised with water? They have received the Holy Spirit just as we have.' So he ordered that they be baptised in the name of Jesus Christ." Acts 10:46-48. He did not ask if they felt like submitting to baptism, he just ordered the baptisms.

The interesting thing is that here we have a case where they had not made a decision outwardly for the Lord Jesus. They were not required to first express any repentance, or receive baptism, but instead at the very preaching of the Gospel, the baptism of the Holy Spirit fell upon them with great power and they all began to speak in tongues. That was because God had prepared the state of their hearts, and God may sovereignly do whatever he desires. He saw within, their heart of faith. He saw within their heart a desire to walk in the truth, and the Holy Spirit came upon them and gave them the whole Gospel conversion experience. All that was left for Peter was to baptise them in water, which he attended to immediately.

Original Church Policy

This New Testament Church practice gave converts a good beginning. They were not in two minds about whether they had made a decision to stand for the Lord Jesus or not. They made a definite response by submitting to the Lord and by submitting to baptism. When you humble yourself to be baptised, this represents a willing obedience to the Lord. When this is done you know you have made a real decision to follow the Lord Jesus Christ.

I hasten to add that the Bible does not teach what is called **"Baptismal Regeneration"**. "Baptismal Regeneration" is an incorrect doctrine that teaches that the actual baptism saves you. It teaches that you must be baptised in water or you are not saved. That you are not born again until, and unless, you are baptised, and that you cannot go to heaven unless you are baptised

But we **DO NOT** believe that. A classic example of the truth is shown in this story of Cornelius. Here was a large group of people, born again to a living hope, filled with the Holy Spirit and who experienced a real saving faith in the Lord. They were born again, redeemed by Jesus Christ, totally renewed, and were *afterwards* baptised. It wasn't the baptism that did the saving work at all, but the grace and power of God alone. Nevertheless, baptism was something that the apostle and the Holy Spirit of God required of them, not for salvation, but for obedience, submission, and public commitment. Even though they had received all the gifts of salvation that God had promised to give them, baptism was still required of them. Though we do not believe in baptismal regeneration, we do believe that submission to baptism is the response we are called to make when God saves us in Christ.

Grace and Faith in Christ Alone

Salvation is by grace and faith alone. When we put our faith in God, his grace comes to us. It is God's grace that saves us. It is our faith in God that provides the state of heart to which his grace comes. Even our faith is a gift from God. There is nothing else we can do to make ourselves acceptable to God. If someone said, *"John, please baptise me,"* and I did so, I could pray and say all the right words, but baptism on its own does not do anything if they do not have a heart of faith in God's saving grace in Christ.

Therefore, I want you to be very clear that we must believe in a salvation by faith alone. We do not believe in baptismal regeneration, but we do believe that baptism goes hand in hand with the proclamation of the Gospel. Baptism is the means God has established for a new believer to respond to the Gospel. When we are baptised in obedience to faith in Christ, having already been saved, some remarkable things do happen in and around our lives, as we shall see in the following chapters.

4
Identification with Christ

"Don't you know that all of us who were baptised into Christ Jesus were baptised into his death? We were therefore buried with him through baptism into death in order that, just as Christ was raised from the dead through the glory of the Father, we too may live a new life. If we have been united with him like this in his death, we will certainly also be united with him in his resurrection."

Romans 6:3-6

Romans Chapter 6 contains a passage where Paul makes some statements concerning the meaning of baptism. What does baptism symbolize? What does it represent when we have a baptism in the Church? What is it a picture of?

The first thing to see from the passage quoted above is that this physical and outward act of baptism is one which identifies us with Christ Himself. Christ died, was buried and rose again, and we are acting that out, in a baptismal ceremony. When a man or woman submits to baptism, they are declaring, "I am identifying myself with the death, the burial, and the resurrection of the Lord Jesus Christ. " It is a particular way of declaring your faith in him, and proclaiming what he has done for you. But you are putting your faith in Jesus, not in the water, for you are saying, "Jesus died, was buried, and rose for me, and I am identifying myself with him".

There are probably other ways in which you could attempt to identify yourself with Christ, but he hasn't established any of them in the Scriptures as being an appropriate act of identification. For example, during the Easter period in the Philippines, there are people who allow themselves to be nailed to a cross as a way of identifying themselves with the events of Calvary. There are also people in the Philippines and other places, who have themselves whipped, but none of these things are an effective means of identifying with Christ. They are not a way to obtain grace. Christ has not set them in the Church. He has not established or ordained them as appropriate ways in which we should identify ourselves with his death, burial and resurrection. But he *has* ordained <u>baptism</u>.

Baptism is also a Christian burial. This is the second aspect of the idea of 'dying' in baptism . When we are baptised, we are laying our old life in a grave. We are putting the old life to death. Not only are we identifying ourselves with what Christ has done, but when we are buried in those waters we are saying that we are dead to the old life. We are dead to our sin. We have left it all behind. And when we are raised up out of the water, we are raised to live a new life, in Christ and for Christ.

Now that we are alive to God, baptism has this two-fold meaning. We identify ourselves with *Christ's* death and resurrection, but we are also testifying by faith to our *own* death, eg: "In Christ I have died. In Christ I have been made alive; I am dead to sin. I have a brand new life. " Colossians 2:12 says, ". . . *having been buried with him in baptism and raised with him through your faith in the power of God, who raised him from the dead.* "

But is baptism only a symbol, or does something actually happen within us? It is apparent that something does happen, and it is very important that it does so. Unseen and often unfelt, baptism is the effective means of cutting off our 'body of sin' and burying it. This is something that concerns our spiritual body and our spiritual life. It relates to the 'spiritual man' and not the natural life that we have. The result however, is that we are 'marked out' before heaven and earth, before angels and demons, as belonging to Christ and somehow the tie that bound us to Satan as the 'god of this world' is broken, and his legal claims on us are removed.

This cutting off of our 'body of sin' and sorting out the legal ownership of our life is of critical importance for us to live in victory. Otherwise, the smell of death and sin often clings to us, and prevents a born-again believer from living in the power, grace and freedom which is their inheritance.

Being 'In Christ'

Central to all the truths and symbols that we find taught in Holy Scripture concerning baptism, and one which is probably the most fundamental and important of all, is that the believer is "in Christ". This is a very powerful and dynamic truth, and the reader is encouraged to study this subject further and to earnestly pray for the Holy Spirit to give you deep insight into your position in Christ. To have a depth of wisdom in this is totally empowering and liberating and will ensure great victory for you as a Christian . It will help you have victory over the world and it's pressures, over the flesh (your sin and human weakness), and over every scheme and resistance of the devil who is your enemy. These things have been defeated and overcome by Christ, and you the believer in Christ will defeat and overcome them also.

You are in Christ because God has placed you there. When you were born again, the Holy Spirit baptised you into one body and placed you in Christ for eternity. This is a finished work and it is your established position. Now by faith you will discover the advantages, the power and the victories of this position. You have been placed in

Christ, joined to the body of Christ and clothed with the righteousness of Christ. From this time on God will see you no other way except as his own. He looks upon you as he looks upon Christ. He loves you as he loves Christ. He will always love you in the same way he loves his only begotten son Jesus. You now belong to the Father as Jesus does. You are part of his family. He has sealed you with his own seal, placed upon you his own name, and in the name of Jesus you have a perfect access to the Father. It is to him you must come with confidence and boldness and you will receive help and grace for all your need.

The apostle Paul wrote many of his letters from prison or during other times of adversity and hardship, but the theme of being 'in Christ' pervades these letters. For Paul, he was not in prison but 'in Christ'. He was not in trouble but 'in Christ'. Thus in his own words *"nothing can separate us from the love of God"* (Romans 8:38), and whatever his circumstances, his life continued to be a channel for the power of God to touch the whole world. It will be the same with you. Victory is not determined by your circumstances but by the way you live and rejoice as an overcomer by faith in Christ.

Being in Christ entitles you to all the benefits of the covenant of God. All the blessings of Abraham are yours, and everything that God has promised. You have all the privileges, all the opportunities, and all the authority of a chosen child of God. The blessings of protection, providence, prosperity, and peace all rest on you. You may freely walk in all that God has said concerning you and all that he has promised you.

In the first two chapters of the book of Ephesians, our high position in Christ is described for us. Here we are told that we died with Christ, we were buried with Christ and then rose with Christ. But something is added which is wonderful and surprising. It tells us that when Christ ascended, we ascended with him, and that Christ is seated at the right hand of the Father and we too are seated there with him. That place is the place of all authority in Heaven and Earth.

The Scripture goes on to teach that Christ is the Head and we are the body, and God the Father has placed all things under the feet of Christ. Even the less important parts of the Body of Christ are above all things. And these things over which we are placed and have authority includes all principalities and powers, all the forces of darkness that would seek to oppose Christ and his people, in advancing the Kingdom of God.

It truly is a wonderful and amazing grace that God has given us who are *'in Christ'*.

5

Putting on Christ

"For all of you who were baptised into Christ, have clothed yourselves with Christ." Galatians 3:27

In baptism we are putting on Christ as our covering or clothing. This 'clothing' is a very important concept in the Bible. Our sins are often referred to as being "rags of unrighteousness" or "filthy rags", but what we receive from Jesus is known as "a robe of righteousness". We are clothed with the righteousness of the Lord Jesus Himself. If we were to rely on our own righteousness, this would never get us to heaven, because you and I have no righteousness of our own. The only way we can ever get to heaven is by trusting in the righteousness of the Lord Jesus Christ.

Galatians 3:27 says that when we are baptised into Christ, we clothe ourselves with him. We put on *his* righteousness.

Notice that this verse makes the statement that we 'clothe ourselves'. This is speaking of the choice we make when we obey the Lord in baptism - we willingly take upon ourselves this great blessing.

The 'Aura' of Christ

I had an unusual experience in 1990. I went to visit a man who had
many problems, weaknesses, and struggles. I knew he was lukewarm,
and a backslider, so I wanted to bring him back to the Lord. I had gone
to visit him after four or five days of fasting, and when sitting down to
talk with him I discovered I was really 'in the Spirit'. He said to me, "*I
made a decision for Christ some years ago and I was baptised, but looking back
on it, I wonder if I didn't just do it because my wife was being baptised. She
made a decision and got baptised and I think that maybe I got baptised because
I was going along with her.*" He was really doubting. He did not know
his own mind any longer. He did not know his own spiritual state.

While he was telling me this, God opened my eyes and I could see in
the Spirit. I saw around this man layers of both light and darkness. I
saw about him, several layers of darkness, each one distinct, one upon
another, representing the problems in his life and the evil that was still
in his heart. Then I saw one really bright layer that was white, pure
clean shining white, and then one more layer of darkness on the
outside. I heard the voice of the Spirit of God say to me, "*You see that
layer of shining white? That is his baptism.*" You see, this man had clothed
himself with Christ.

Baptism had been for him an act of true faith at the time, even
though he was later struggling with his thoughts and feelings. He had
received the Lord Jesus, and had been buried with Christ in baptism.
Even though he was now in a backslidden state, God had never
removed that seal from him, for he believed in Jesus. He still had upon
him this precious mark, the seal of God which was the righteousness of
Christ, given to him as a gift. When I saw the gift of God on this man
who had been baptised and clothed with the righteousness of Christ, I
was able to assure him and see him restored to peace, and a walk with
God.

You cannot earn this gift. If you think that you must have a certain
state of cleanness before you can have righteousness from Christ, it isn't

so. It is a gift, and cannot be earned or obtained by deserving it. Of course, once you do receive it, the call of God is to then live out that righteousness in how you think and act day by day, by the power of the Holy Spirit, and to actually become a holy person. Your goal is to become Christ-like. Nevertheless, the gift is given by God's grace alone in response to your faith.

Righteousness as a Gift

Central to the Gospel of Jesus Christ is this truth that when you place your faith in the saving work of Jesus Christ on the Cross, and trust him alone to be your Saviour and deliverer, then God gives to you his grace. This is a free and undeserved gift, of his *righteousness* which you need in order to be holy. You need to be in right standing with God. You need to be acceptable to God. You need to be considered clean. To be righteous means to be good and holy and to be pure and clean. This change occurs within you at the moment you receive the gift of his righteousness.

The human mind cannot fathom how righteousness could be given as a gift, especially to people who have never been righteous and have no hope of making themselves righteous.

Our minds can understand receiving other things as gifts, like an inheritance for example. We hear of people receiving a house, or a million dollars, or other good things, given to them in some benefactor's Will. In Christ we do have an inheritance, and through the will of the Father we become joined to Christ, and inherit the righteousness of the Son of God, something for which we do not have to work. We cannot buy it, we cannot earn it, we cannot deserve it. Indeed God the Father will only give it on the condition that we do not attempt to earn it or deserve it, but are willing to receive it as a freely given gift of grace.

This is a very good position from which to begin our relationship with God. It means that from the first day we do not strive to be good enough for God but we are at peace with him. We are at rest and completely secure in our relationship with him. This is important because the goal of that relationship is for us to find intimacy with God the Father and the Son. There cannot be intimacy except in a secure relationship. If the relationship was based on demands or rules, and our being good enough, intimacy would not be found. But intimacy is what God Himself is looking for with you. And so he brings you into a secure relationship with Himself, one in which intimacy and love can grow – because of your complete acceptance by God and being righteous in his eyes.

Subjects such as righteousness, intimacy with God, being In Christ, grace, and the power of the indwelling Spirit are of such magnitude and of such wonder that they will occupy your exploring heart and give you growth in faith and joy the rest of your life upon earth, and for all of eternity.

6

Baptised into one Body

"For we were all baptised by one Spirit into one body whether Jews or Greeks, slave or free, and we were all given the one Spirit to drink." 1 Corinthians 12:13

Here is a passage of Scripture which shows that, when joined to Christ and having been given the Spirit of God, *we were brought into a relationship with all other believers*. This is not just an ordinary relationship such as an earthly friendship, but we have actually been joined by God into a single body. We must understand that when we are baptised into Christ, we are baptised into the Body of Christ. Our baptism represents the fact that we have come into relationship with Christ, and that we have also come into a relationship with Christ's people. As a result of baptism, and what baptism represents, you and I have a very clear and distinct relationship with one another, as well as with Christ. He is our Head, and we all make up his body. Together we are Christ on earth.

This means that we have responsibilities toward one another and that there should be a commitment in our hearts to each other. This is why the Scripture says, "*Submit yourselves to one another out of reverence*

for Christ" and *"do not forsake the assembling of yourselves together.
"* (Ephesians 5:21 and Hebrews 10:25.) We need to see that there is a definite relationship that we are able to develop and enjoy when we are in Christ.

Ephesians 4:3-6 says, *"Make every effort to keep the unity of the Spirit through the bond of peace. There is one body and one Spirit, just as you were called to one hope when you were called; one Lord, one faith, one baptism, one God and Father of all who is over all and through all and in all. "* Within this passage that speaks so much about unity and oneness, and of keeping the unity of the Spirit in the bond of peace, it is stated that *"one baptism"* is part of this foundation for the unity of the Body.

This confirms the Scripture from 1 Corinthians 12 which declares that when you are baptised into Christ you are baptised into his Body, the church of the living God. Praise the Lord.

New Believers Become Part of the Body

It is so important that the new believer, and every believer, sees himself or herself as being an integral and important part of the church. The church is the Body of Christ, and is on earth to do the work of Christ. All believers together are the Body of Christ, but this is expressed in each place by a local church.

Each believer should be a dedicated, faithful, caring and praying member of a vital Christian fellowship. Do you want to learn, mature, and discover your full inheritance and destiny? You will do this in meaningful relationships with other Christians under anointed leadership. A good local church will be full of life and love - believing the Bible, praying with faith, preaching Jesus and committed to discovering and doing the will of God. Your own blessing and fulfillment, as well as your encouragement and safety, is mainly established by being in a committed relationship with other believers. You need the Church and the fellowship of the saints as an essential part of the life you live for Christ.

Relationships Within the Body

Experience has shown that most of the blessings which come to us as Christians come to us only when we are in relationship with other believers and are submitted to anointed leaders in the Body of Christ. The blessings are promised, and the fullness of our inheritance is available to us, but some believers miss out on much that is their inheritance, either because they have an independent spirit, or they have never been taught about how to walk with the Lord in relationship with other believers. When we come into our Christ-ordained relationship with the local church, we will more easily understand and obtain the fullness of his promises and the blessings which are the inheritance of Christ for us, and which are freely available.

It is God's desire for us to be in proper relationship with other believers, and we will grow and mature in the wisdom of Christ. But when believers do not love the other believers, or have an independent spirit, they invariably become hard, their relationship with Christ seems to die away, and their faith becomes small. Very often these people live in darkness and in bondage even though they have laid claim to the blessings of Christ. We must avoid at all cost an independent spirit or an unteachable attitude, and we must see that the blessings and the life of Christ are present and available to us when we have a right attitude to, and relationship with, other believers. The Apostle John said *"He who says he loves God but does not love his brother is a liar; for he who does not love his brother whom he has seen, cannot love God whom he has not seen.* " 1 John 4:20.

Your faithful Christian life will be a life lived in love; love for Christ, for your fellow believers, and even for your enemies. As you walk with Jesus He will teach you how to love others, how to serve others, how to be willing to lay down your life that others will be blessed. A Godly love is a selfless attitude of heart which always desires the highest good for the other person and which will love even when love is not returned. In the end, the life of learning to love as God loves is the most important part of being transformed into the image of Christ. The qualities of this life will be with you for eternity.

7
A Promise to God

"God waited patiently in the days of Noah while the ark was being built. In it only a few people, eight in all, were saved through water, and this water symbolises baptism that now saves you also - not the removal of dirt from the body, but the pledge of a good conscience towards God. It saves you by the resurrection of Jesus Christ." 1 Peter 3:20-21

Baptism is a promise to God. When a person submits to baptism, they are making a pledge from their heart in good faith to serve God. From the significant passage of Scripture above, we draw an important truth. It states that the flood which carried Noah in the ark to safety, symbolises baptism. What was significant about that flood is that the same water which destroyed a multitude, also saved the elect. It was the same water, but the ark was the ark of salvation. Now the Church, which is the Body of Christ, is the ark of our salvation, and the water of baptism is an important symbol that represents our being in the ark of salvation.

A key issue in this passage is found in the phrase that says, *"not the removal of dirt from the body, but the pledge of a good conscience toward God.*

" It means this: The power or the effectiveness of baptism is not in the water that washes. The water is physical and tangible, but the power in baptism is not found in the water itself.

Rather the power of baptism is in *'the pledge of a good conscience toward God'*. In other words, it is not the water itself that draws power from God in baptism, but the state of the heart of the person who enters the water. If someone seeks baptism but enters the water with a wrong heart attitude toward God, (ie without faith) nothing positive can happen - they merely get wet. But if someone goes into the water of baptism with a right heart toward God, then the Spirit of God does a wonderful and powerful work. Something happens as a result of that baptism. Something is happening in that person's life, and the Scripture says it's the result of the pledge of a good conscience toward God, which means you're making a promise to live according to the principles that your baptism represents. You're saying, "Lord, this is my definite, outward and public way of saying 'THIS IS IT! I'm Yours forever, and I'm holding nothing back'. " In the pledge of a good conscience toward God, we find that baptism has power. Without the pledge of a good conscience, it's only water.

The Removal of Satan's Claim

Some years ago the Rev. David Pawson told the story of an outstanding event which took place in his church in England. A young man who had been a motorcycle gang member, was converted. He had come in with leather jacket and studs, covered with tattoos all over his body, found the Lord Jesus, and was soundly converted. He loved the Lord whole-heartedly, and under the guidance of those good people he wanted to be baptised. Unfortunately, he had upon his chest an ugly tattoo of the devil, a dreadful satanic face. And he realised that when he was baptised wearing the white shirt that was customary to wear in that church, the shirt would become transparent and he would come up out of the water with this image of the devil showing on his chest.

Understandably, he didn't want that! He wanted to deal with the tattoo before getting baptised, so he went to the doctor to find out what could be done. To have it surgically removed would have cost him around £3,000 - which he could not afford. He didn't have anywhere near that amount of money. So he sought the Lord in prayer and felt strongly that he should be baptised anyway.

He felt he should not put if off, but should simply yield to baptism as he was. When they baptised him one Sunday morning, he went down into the water with that tattoo on his chest and came up out of the water - minus one tattoo! It was gone - completely washed off by the grace and power of God in the waters of baptism! The Lord granted a wonderful miracle. The faith of the heart of this man toward God had called forth that miracle, and Christ had used this occasion to show not only his power over all things, but how the pledge of a good conscience in baptism removes Satan's claim and mark upon our lives.

In your baptism into Christ a deep work of the Spirit takes place. This is not only symbolic, but both within and about us the power of Christ is at work, dealing with our hearts and the spirit world around us.

Please take note of this: A real cleansing, a real washing, *does* take place in the Spirit. Something that is beyond our understanding takes place as God removes from our lives many things that cling to us.

8
A Public Witness

"If you confess with your mouth Jesus is Lord and believe in your heart God raised him from the dead, you will be saved. For it is with your heart that you believe and are justified, and it is with your mouth that you confess and are saved."

Romans 10:9

Baptism is a public witness. The importance of making a public confession of faith must be stressed, because it is essential to your faith and your experience of God. You will not find the word 'baptism' in the text above, but you do find something that is critical to your strength as a Christian , and which is very much related to baptism into Christ

The Scripture speaks about <u>believing</u> in your heart and <u>confessing</u> with your mouth. You might think that believing with your heart and confessing with your mouth is basically the same thing, but there is a big difference, and they each have something to do with your being saved. (Verse 10) *"It is with your heart that you believe and are justified. It is with your mouth that you confess and are saved. "* What is the difference between being justified (which is the result when you believe), and being saved (which is the outcome of confession) ?

I want you to know that when you confess with your mouth what you believe, something *more* takes place in you than what happens when you believe without making an open confession of it.

Justification is a word that speaks about your relationship with God. If we say that you are justified, it means that you have come into a right relationship with him. You have placed your faith in God. He has forgiven your sins. You have eternal life. You will go to heaven. Jesus is your Saviour and Lord. You have been justified, made right with God.

But to be *saved* means more than that. The word that has been translated as 'saved' also means 'healed' or 'delivered'. There is much more that should come to you after you've been forgiven. Forgiveness is wonderful, but you need to be set free from the *power* of your sin. You must be delivered from it, and healed of its effects.

For example, someone may have an addiction to drugs or to alcohol. God can forgive them, but they may still be addicted. But if you are *saved,* (healed, delivered) you are set free from that addiction. Do you see the difference? You may be in bondage to dirty thoughts. You may be in bondage to bitterness, or hatred, or to some other iniquity that is in your life. To receive forgiveness is one thing, but to receive deliverance is another.

So if you want more than forgiveness, you have got to do more than just believe with your heart. If you want to be completely set free from your sin, if you want to begin living the new life in it's fullness, if you want to come into all the benefits that healing, wholeness, salvation and deliverance bring, then it will be on the basis of your confession. You will need to speak openly words that express your faith in Christ, and give a clear testimony to the fact that you trust him alone as the Saviour of your life.

The Scripture says that if you believe in your heart, you will be justified, but when you confess with your mouth, you will be saved -

you will be set free, you will be delivered! You will come into a full experience of all that God has for you. This is one of the reasons why people make a confession when they are baptised. They declare their faith in the Lord Jesus, saying "I believe Jesus has died for my sins. I believe that my sins are washed away. Now I'm living for Jesus. " This is a public confession of faith. The word of God says that such a confession of faith brings power to deliver. It has power to set you free. You will find that blessing flows upon your life every time you testify concerning the Saviour and share the goodness of the Lord Jesus with others.

Believers' Baptism and Infant Baptism

Consider now two things about the practice of public baptism. *Firstly,* baptism is meant to be a believer's baptism rather than the sprinkling of infants, for baptism is our willing submission to the Lordship of Christ. The sprinkling of infants is not really baptism at all, and you will not find the concept of baptising babies anywhere in the Scriptures, although the Jewish practice of the dedication of infants is upheld and honoured in the gospel story of Jesus' own life. Of course, young people and children who have come to know the Lord and confess to know his salvation may be, and should be, baptised as believers.

There are reasons why it should be a believer's baptism. Chief amongst them is that baptism requires conversion, a born again experience, which has within it the two elements of regeneration and repentance. Regeneration is something that God works in you, and repentance is something that you express in coming to God. To be converted requires regeneration, i. e. the Holy Spirit must come to you and awaken your heart, so that you are alive to God. Conversion also requires your repentance, i. e. your response to God, saying, "I give up my old life. I turn from my sins and I turn to You. " Baptism by it's very nature requires a believer to experience these two things - regeneration and repentance - but an infant or an as-yet unbelieving child, has not experienced them.

This is not saying that little children are not in the Kingdom of God. Of course they are! We believe the word of the Lord Jesus when he says that *"of such is the Kingdom of Heaven"*. Without doubt any child who dies in infancy goes to be with the Lord. Whether the parents are Christian or not, I believe that God has his hand upon each child. You cannot alter the state of salvation of babies by baptising them. The faith of the parents does help, it's true, but it is of special help for every child that lives! In presenting a child to God saying, "Lord, we thank You for this child. We ask that You put Your hand upon this child, and we dedicate this child to You, etc", the dedication of believing parents really does bring a blessing on a child for life.

Christening (infant baptism) does not do more for babies than dedication, but New Testament baptism upon conversion is wonderfully effective for the believer. Baptism requires faith, obedience, submission, the pledge of the heart toward God, and confession of the Lord Jesus. An infant being sprinkled does not bring any of these things to baptism, and thus is not really baptised at all, for these things are the essence of the works of grace which are brought to a place of focus, decision and experience in our submission to the Lord's command.

Secondly, baptism is best by full immersion whenever possible. The Jews who used this idea first, forbade even hair ribbons and the clenching of fists in case some part of the body might not be touched with the water.

John the Baptist used the springs near Salim to baptise because there was plenty of water there **(John 3:23)**. He needed a lot of water for complete immersion of the repentant person. Jesus' disciples also baptised in the same place.

The Scriptures hold another reason why immersion is genuinely important. Baptism represents death, burial, and resurrection. If we only *sprinkle* with water, this representation of being buried and raised again, is missing. Sprinkling may represent washing, but immersion presents a full picture of washing, burial, and resurrection as well.

A book called "The Didache", which means "The Teaching", published by the church in AD 100, taught total immersion. That was the practice of the early church. Professor Karl Bath, a great reformed scholar and one of the most famous theologians of recent times said, "Primitive baptism (meaning baptism in it's most earliest form in the church), had the characteristic of a direct threat to life, succeeded immediately by deliverance and preservation".

But finally, the very meaning of the word itself, points to immersion. The word "baptise", or to "be baptised", means to immerse, to plunge, to sink, to overwhelm. This is why we baptise by immersion. However, we should never reject or think lightly of the baptism of someone who has submitted to believer's baptism in some other form, and for whom this was their submission to follow Christ on the confession of their faith.

A story is told of the church in revival in Africa. During a time of terrible drought, when there was no spare water anywhere, converts were being baptised into Christ by lying down in the dust and having dust thrown on them. There are times when necessity requires Holy Spirit 'invention', and I believe this story is of a most suitable baptism, which will come with all the blessings ordained by God.

9
Obedience to Christ

"Jesus came to them and said, 'All authority in heaven and on earth has been given to me. Therefore, go and make disciples of all nations, baptising them in the name of the Father and of the Son and of the Holy Spirit, and teaching them to obey everything I have commanded you and surely I am with you always. '"

Matthew 28:18-20

I have left until last a discussion of this most important aspect of baptism, which is, obedience to Jesus Christ. Here is a plain command from the lips of Jesus - "<u>Go and make disciples, baptise them and teach them to obey</u>! " With baptism, we should not wait until a person has a conviction that they ought to be baptised. Jesus says, "Teach them to obey. " The mandate upon the church is to instruct every person, saying to them, "Jesus says you should be baptised. "

We need to obey him in this, and we need to teach new believers obedience. We have a brother in our church who came under conviction regarding baptism, but because of his medical condition, put it off time and time again. He was trying to find some way to prevent the medical appliance which was taped to his body from coming off when he was immersed. There seemed to be no solution to the problem and, continuing to put his baptism off over many months, the end result was that his heart grew cold, and he began to avoid the issue of baptism. Nine months went by, and he was not doing well spiritually, and there seemed a lack of blessing on the circumstances of his family, finances and emotions. Knowing that he previously had held a deep conviction about baptism, I went to him one day and said, "You are just messing things up. You have come under condemnation because you have put off what was a conviction of the Holy Spirit in your heart". He recognised that what I said was truth. He knew I was right and so we baptised him two Sundays later. He said to me afterwards, "I had been praying many prayers for long months. I have had many problems and a lot of needs, so I prayed, and prayed, and prayed, but just couldn't get my prayers answered. But the very week following my baptism, I have had all those prayers answered. "

You see! When we put off what God calls us to do, we bring ourselves under the condemnation of the enemy, and bring ourselves into bondage. When we obey, whether we feel like obeying or not, we bring grace upon our lives. This is why the Lord Jesus said, *"make disciples. . . teaching them to obey"*, and we ought to be obedient in the matter of baptism first of all. This is an act of obedience all of us are called to make.

A Summary of what Baptism Means

1. Submitting to baptism is part of fulfilling all righteousness. To be baptised is to do the will of God.

2. Baptism is purposely joined by God to the substance and meaning of our conversion (our re-birth in Christ).

3. It is identifying ourselves with Christ's death, burial and resurrection, and at the same time we, by faith, have died to our old life, rising to a new life in Christ.

4. It is putting on Christ and his righteousness.

5. It is being baptised into the Body of Christ, and so in Christ we are united with all other believers (the church).

6. It is the pledge of a good conscience toward God. This is a commitment.

7. It is a public witness. We make the confession that brings the greater experience of salvation and deliverance.

8. It is obedience to Christ. Those not obedient to Christ in baptism, having been informed concerning it, often prove to be disobedient in other matters also.

Demonic reaction against Baptism

I have discovered by experience that Satan hates baptism. Indeed, in many nations of this world there is often a violent reaction from the relatives of people who turn to Christ from pagan and godless religions. Usually the greatest reaction is not over their reading the Bible or saying that they believe in Jesus, but over their decision to be baptised. This is the reaction of religious spirits seeking to maintain control over that family or that society. This in itself is evidence that there is a tremendous power in baptism.

In Conclusion

We do not fully understand what God does in baptism. Even though some people seem to have all that is necessary before we baptise them, we do believe that when baptised, God does an important and mystical work within them – a work that is essential. We do not teach that it is essential for salvation and eternal life (because we receive that by grace alone), but we *do* believe it is essential for obedience. It is essential for a more perfect walk in the Holy Spirit, and essential for receiving the fullness of deliverance for the earthly life. It is a physical, symbolic and outward act, but your heart in submission and obedience to Christ will receive much blessing through this wonderful means of grace.

The Ethiopian said to Philip, *"What is to keep me from being baptised?"* Acts 8:36,37.

Ananias said to Saul, *"What are you waiting for? Get up, be baptised and wash your sins away, calling on his name."* Acts 9:17.

What about you? Have *you* obeyed the Lord Jesus? What is to hinder *you* from being baptised?

"Get up! " the word of God says, "What are you waiting for? Get up and be baptised. Wash away your sins. " If you have no other sin, you have at least this sin - the sin of disobedience to the Word of God in this matter. Get up, wash away your sins, calling upon his name.

Although obeying the religious concepts of man and human institutions brings people into bondage and dryness, obeying Jesus releases us and brings us into freedom. Jesus said, *"If you continue in my word, then you are truly my disciples, and you will know the truth, and the truth will set you free."* John 8:31-32.

We do not serve the Lord in a legalistic spirit, but we respond to a knowledge of his will with a glad heart. The evidence of being a Christian is that we love, and have a desire to obey the Lord, and seek to know his will.

Holy Scripture says: *"In keeping his commands there is great reward"* Psalm 19:11, and the response of the true believer is *"I delight to do Your will, O God. "* Psalm 40:8.

10

The Preparation of Your Heart for Baptism

Charles Haddon Spurgeon, known as the 'Prince of Preachers' and considered to be the greatest preacher of all time, told his personal experience of baptism:

"I can never forget 3rd May, 1850; it was my mother's birthday, and I myself within a few weeks of being sixteen years of age. I was up early to have a couple of hours for quiet prayer and dedication to God. Then I had some eight miles to walk, to reach the spot where I was to be immersed into the Triune Name according to the sacred command.

"The wind blew down the river with a cutting blast, as my turn came to wade into the flood, but after I had walked a few steps and noted the people on the ferry-boat, and in boats, and on either shore, I felt as if Heaven, and earth, and hell, might all gaze upon me, for I was not ashamed, there and then, to own myself a follower of the Lamb. My timidity was washed away; it floated

*down the river into the sea, and must have been devoured by the
fishes, for I have never felt anything of the kind since.*
*"Baptism also loosed my tongue and from that day it has never
been quiet. I lost a thousand fears in that River Lark, and found
that 'in keeping his commandments there is great reward'. "*

C. H. Spurgeon, The Early Years 1834-1859
Banner of Truth, page 149

Spurgeon built a great congregation in London and raised many
other works for God. His teachings have been used, and continue to be
used, across the nations to this present day. God took a shy young man
and filled him with grace and power. This He will do with everyone
whose heart is fully dedicated to Jesus Christ. Baptism is the sign and
symbol of this dedication.

I am greatly moved by this account of Spurgeon's baptism. When I
read his words *"I lost a thousand fears in that River Lark"*, I feel deep love
for God. I know how good the Lord is, not only to Spurgeon, but to
uncounted millions of people who know his name. The Lord is good
and the knowledge of his love is wonderful. I yearn for you, my fellow
believer, my brother or sister, that by faith you might obtain every
blessing and benefit for which Christ has died, and that your
knowledge of the Lord would be sweet, enjoying the intimacy with
Jesus that is available to you.

Spurgeon also wrote: *"I was up early to have a couple of hours for quiet
prayer and dedication to God"* before being *"immersed into the triune name
according to the sacred command"*.

Each believer should do as Spurgeon did, and approach their
submission and surrender to Christ in baptism with devotion and
seriousness, with a purposeful preparation of the heart. Then the
power of his grace would be so much more revealed in them.

In keeping his commands there is great reward. You should prepare your heart for Baptism by seeking God's face, renouncing pride, embracing humility, seeking a deeper cleansing of the heart and a more perfect knowledge of the will of God.

At this point remember that in coming to God your main goal is to focus on Jesus. Don't keep the focus of prayer only on yourself, your own needs and your own faults. It is Him you seek to know - this is what you hunger for.

You should come to the place of full and complete surrender of your will, your love and all your desires to Jesus Christ. Searching the scriptures will help you find Him.

It is when we die to ourselves that we find great gain. He who dies to self shall find a truly better life. Only in Christ is your great reward. I commend you now to the grace of God who alone can make you perfect. Remember, by His grace and your faith, even your weaknesses will become a strength.

For more resources by
John Alley visit
peace.org.au